Contents

Time

Bridie is gone
and Charlie is gone.

Bridget is gone
and Kay is gone.

Bernard is gone
and Bill is gone.

Kathleen is gone
and Chrissie is gone.

Michael is gone
and Mac is gone.

Nan is gone
and so is Maura.

Bridie: quiet dutiful dependent and young
stricken with cancer, went peacefully
supported by family intercession and Extreme Unction.

Charlie: for a long time a bulwark against the laws of nature
succumbed, jaundiced by the rigours of tobacco and alcohol.
His widow, penniless, but with eleven children,
helped him to go peacefully
supported by family intercession and Extreme Unction.

Bridget: strong willed in her youth,
and frail in extreme old age, died, blind and senile.
Long dead was her industry and thrift.
Long dead was her warmth and curiosity.
Long dead was her religious devotion.
But living still, is Grandma,
who didn't need Extreme Unction.

Kay: a recluse, went at the right time for Kay.
Having given as much as she could, she went peacefully,
supported by family intercession and Extreme Unction.
She knew both the joys and sorrows of love,
and the joys and sorrows of childbirth,
and familiar with the rigour of work,
walked the streets at night in despair -
when the Blue Pool, was synonymous with thoughts of suicide.

Bernard: full of fun in his youth, and a scholar,
went after a tantrum with his doctor,
who was at least as strong willed:
"No more driving Bernard!" was the edict.
Bernard spoke fondly of: "The Almighty,"
and was prone to giving advice.

Bill: an old IRA man, philosopher, and saint, died,
but not before raising himself up and saluting his God.
Quiet, and a provider of daughters,
he prayed, unceasing, for his comrades,
for those they fought against, and especially,
those who died.

Kathleen died: where many paupers had lived,
in Nazareth House,
and mercifully before her legs were amputated.
"A sight!" with her grey wizened head and dishevelled garb,
her ambition was to be off - somewhere! anywhere!
No apple tart could equal her apple tart,
nor seasoned keg rival her frying pan for flavour.
Her laugh was uproarious, and her piety plain.
And her weakness was to be in awe of others.

Chrissie: with her infectious laugh and soft charm, is gone.
Hospitality was preferably out of doors, in a warm snug;
the gateway to which, was a discrete door in off the street.
No farmer could have wished for a better crop of sons.

No housewife was less hurried, more tolerant or forgiving.
And nobody was more surprised, than all of us,
when she died from a heart attack.

Michael: stout, soft spoken and gentle, knew every face in the town
and townland, for he had been, and still was, "The Master."
A wise man, he never let his learning escape, preferring his pipe.
He could talk to his sons, as you would talk to a friend,
and everyone liked him.
He died in bed, and sadly, before Cavan
could thrash their opponents at football, that afternoon.
In the church - it was standing room only.

A wiry man, Mac is gone, and thankfully, before
in his old age, he had to use his bucket of water and garden fork
against marauding and murderous Loyalist gangs.
What an indignity, and cruel twist of fate that would have been
for a Squadron Leader, who, in his youth, defended the nation.

A devoted mother and welcoming host,
Nan, with her unnerving worldly wisdom, is gone.
A lingering death, she was cared for to the end,
and is at peace.

Professional, patriotic, cultured and refined,
Maura, in all her complexity, is gone. Her life:
the embodiment of confused piety, thwarted ambition and pain.
At fifty, she learned to drive. And at sixty three left home
for one of her own, paying cash.
Always overweight and a lover of chocolate, she died,
age ninety five, but not before telling them, in the operating theatre,
of Derry, "in the long ago," and of what she was most proud of.
A life spent teaching, "the poorest of the poor."
at the Long Tower Girl's School

And I stand - here!

Time - A Sequel

In the fading light of a dank December evening,
and, as a stranger, I left the High Street,
preferring instead to find an oasis of calm on the hillside.
Slowly, I climbed past forgotten headstones,
some upright, some tottering, and some laid low,
until high above the mossed tree trunks,
birds, like children, frantically twittered.
Beyond and more defiant still, stood the dumb church,
its duelled towers and distended shape,
a vulgar and sinister testament.
Gone now, was the incessant noise of traffic,
the thump of drums, clang of symbols, and the barmy
and pantomime laughter of children.
And there in front of me were the twins,
Paul and David.
Loved by their parents.
And recently dead.

Paul, who had lived for "41 hours."
And David,
who had lived for "2 ½ hours."

And there, in the damp and fading light,
I saw it proclaimed, as truth!
That love is eternal.
And that Time - is never past.

Bad Timing ?

It was February and cold.
Outside the grey ocean raged against the rocks.
Inside, it was warm, even plush.

Subdued we were on the landing,
when a deferential voice passed up the news,
that the hearse had arrived.

In an instant, the coffin was in the hallway below.
And as it resolutely ascended the stairs,
the house, in the presence of death,
shrivelled.

And when every emotion was crushed,
and death at the head of the stairs - triumphant!
there was a loud explosion.
It was the telephone
ringing with vulgarity.
Instinctively I throttled it, but a voice said:
"Hello, is that Dalriada?"
"Yes".
"We would like to book a holiday for the Easter Weekend."
"I'm sorry, but we are in family mourning."

Back on the landing, I was in time to see the coffin
making its way down the narrow passage to its resting place..
And as I watched, I thought,
how extraordinary the hand of fate.
Since she, who would have made the holiday,
was in the coffin.

Miss Mills

Miss Mills, a spinster,
came around to our house,
and in deep tones, and in her smock,
talked and laughed about whatever it was
that women talked and laughed about,
when they were shut in
and we were locked out.

And when I on an errand
went around to Miss Mills house,
and stood in her kitchen,
bathed as it was in soft evening sunlight,
and returned home perplexed,
and telling my mother the news,
that Miss Mills was icing a wedding cake!
My mother told me that Miss Mills was getting married.

Miss Mills lived in "Belvedere":
"A house on a height with steps up to it
and a beautiful view."
So when in the cool of evening
and with the sea behind me,
I climbed the steep steps to Belvedere,
it wasn't as a wedding guest, but a fledgling,
thoughtfully invited to the remnants of the feast.

Always in her apron, and always busy,
Miss Mills, with her deep tones and hearty laugh,
was always welcoming, and always kind,
and her home, always a place of order.
No prying questions were ever asked.
No prophetic judgements given. Nothing
that could disturb the peace of a small boy's mind.
To Miss Mills, you were always *you*.

As when in the dead of night,
and fearing torment from alcohol,
we were roused from our warm beds
and in the darkness, climbed the steep steps
to that house with a beautiful view,
and passed like shadows into the floodlit stairwell,
to warm beds in safe rooms,
Miss Mills was elsewhere.

As when our mother cried in pain,
and the priest sent for, came to countermand the lie,
and all of them were "bitches,
the whole bloody lot of them."
And when every bottle had been dredged and double-dredged
and the boy guarded the man lest he fell into the fire,
then I knew, in my stoical brain, the true worth,
of that house, on that height, with steps up to it,
and its beautiful view.

A policeman, Chris was as tall as Maud was small,
and quiet, and gentle, and soft.

Maud was a Protestant.
Maud was an ex. Salvationist
And Maud was a saint

Who would be a girl when you can be a boy ?

Who would be a girl when you can be a boy
and run about with your hair standing on end
with your nose dirty and glasses twisted,
and with one sock up and with one sock down,
and knees: "black as the ace of spades" ?

Who would be a girl when you can be a boy
and on your way to school, play with guns and caps,
fill water-pistols down the toilet
and dash out into the playground
spraying friend and foe alike?

Who would be a girl when you can be a boy
oblivious to time, traffic, and passers by,
and with one foot on the pavement, and the other in the road,
make your way home from school - backwards,
playing marbles, all the way home?

Who would be a girl when you can be a boy
and second in command in the Harbour Gang.
And with your coat fastened at the neck,
run Batman-like through the streets?
And woe-betide any other gang.

Who would be a girl when you can be a boy
and for a month plan bonfire night, scouring
shops and alleys, and dragging home from garages
tyres as big and heavy as yourself. And with your friend
keep lookout, for raiding parties that never arrive?

Who would be a girl when you can be a boy
and be really really really smart!
and jump into bed with your clothes on,
so that you don't have to bother
with getting dressed in the morning?

Who would be a girl when you can be a boy
and watch men at work, especially with steam rollers,
and be a fish-mongers' helper on a Saturday
without mother knowing, get paid,
and run home, sniffing your jumper with pride?

Who would be a girl when you can be a boy
and, sensing the majesty of ships on the sea,
know, that it is your destiny to be a sailor.
And sit alone on the rocks, your heart aching
as "Vanguard" and "St. Kits", silently, move away?

Who would be a girl when you can be a boy
and single handed and fearless, rescue your teacher
from certain death and swell with pride
when the teacher, mentioning you, explains to the confused,
the difference between a lumber-jacket and a lumber-jack?

Who would be a girl when you can be a boy
and stuff your head with knowledge when going shopping,
and flaunt it shamelessly, item, by item,
while the girl behind the counter smiles at you lovingly,
and news of your mental prowess, becomes a local legend?

Who would be a girl when you can be a boy,
and fall in love with girls?

Paddy Johnson

Unexpected and unannounced
and always through the back door,
he appeared in the captive den;
and we were in awe and glad.
This silent leathery creature,
this mystic, with his tattoos picked out in India,
who brought renewed life, renewed hope,
and youthfulness to mother's features.
Slack of posture and sleek of foot
and with no time to barter,
Paddy, who still was what he had always been,
took his place in the mess.

"Breakfast for Two."
"No! Two adults and one child,
three breakfasts."
"Out of the way!"
"Yes, toast, lots of toast!"
"Can someone see to these dirty dishes
they're piling up like crazy?"
"No! Mr. Weir hasn't appeared yet."
"Here! Give that teapot a wipe, its filthy!
And you! upstairs, scrub your face
and wash behind your ears."

And all this while, Paddy -
silent and attentive in the background.

Potatoes peeled, yet again!
Lunches served, yet again!
Dishes, and pots and pans washed, yet again!
Floors scrubbed, yet again!
And the deep-fat fryer stirring.

And all this while the sun, barely noticed,
creeping from East to West,
until a shimmer of light on the dusted window
makes less bleak
the high wall opposite.
And mother, deprived of the sea view,
the golden sand, and the long arm of the Giant's Causeway,
delights, in a few wallflowers.

Then with suppers served, and lovers
and would-be lovers heading for the dance,
and children, toppled by the waves, exhausted and asleep,
Paddy, alone at the kitchen table, studies "form";
until fearing our bedtime, and by entreaty, he recalls
hot sun, strange insects, snake charmers, and bayonets,
while rolling a cigarette, tapping it end to end
and placing it in readiness behind his ear.
Then, in our very own kitchen, and just for us,
he chews razor blades, swallows and spits fire,
and for an encore, with a frantic moving of his wrinkled hand
twangs the Jew's Harp into life.

Unexpected and unannounced
and, always through the back gate
and down the dreary lane,
he would escape this captive den;
and we were ponderous and sad.

This silent leathery creature;
this mystic with his tattoos picked out in India,
who, having come from nowhere,
was gone nowhere, but,
who in his going, was everywhere.
In the shining black-leaded range.
In the hot coals glowing with an intensity not noticed before.
And in the plates, stacked ready for breakfast.

And when I, standing on the steps, inspected the brasses,
gleaming in the morning light, I sensed,
that only the dawn, and Paddy,
knew of his secret.

"What will be will be."
A poem in defence of nuns
and for all those who deserved better.

I went there, and until my dying day will regret,
that I ever heard of the place.
But as the song said, "What will be will be."
And my name is there on a plaque on the wall.
And no experience is an entirely bad experience.
For it to be bad, good has to be present, somewhere.

And I rubbed shoulders with the great:
two cardinals, before either of them knew that
"What will be will be."
And I sang solo for Sir Malcolm Sergeant
before most of you had heard of him.
And I was a silent witness to a miracle in the Philharmonic Hall,
where a man with a stick knew how to use it.

As we left, I knew that the roughneck from Crossmaglen
had been on the road to Damascus.
Undaunted by the eloquence of the orchestra,
this country yokel had opened his soul
to, "The Flight of the Bumble Bee".
And when he turned up in school with a melodeon
and didn't know what to do, and I taught him to play,
he took off like a bee, and, flitting from tune to tune,
within weeks was better than me.

We went to New Brighton when New Brighton was a place worth going to.
And to Chester, on an outing sponsored by a benefactor,
whom the nuns feared wouldn't be a benefactor, after some of us,
forgetting our manners, made pigs of ourselves in a posh hotel.

On a good day you couldn't tell the difference
between St Vincent's and Bedlam.
The corridors were long and cold, and slamming doors,
together with the incessant and discordant sound of pianos,
echoed, and re-echoed, through the place.
In their spare time the Irish fought the English.
And one boy, disturbed by things other than his blindness,
poking his fingers into his eyes, rocked mournfully to and fro.
While the twins, blind and newly arrived,
and separated from their mother for the first time,
cried pitifully for days.
John cried out for "Joe". And Joe cried out for "John."

It was a mad place!
A school and convent rolled into one,
with the sacred and profane cohabiting.
And where the nuns, taking prolonged refuge in the chapel
once a month, emerged refreshed. But,
"What will be will be."
and in the evenings as they prepared for school,
it was to the strains of Paul Anka's
knowing and orgasmic lyrics booming down the corridor.
"Thrills I get when you hold me close. Oh! Diana! you're the most."
But if it was a mad, mad, place, "thanks be to God"
there was only one "mad nun" in it.

But tell me God, why, after everything else, I had to endure her.
That demented soul, who, with her brood gathered, and coronet wagging,
told us, more than once, that the happiest day of her life
would be the day of her death.
But meantime, and with no less fervour,
she killed the spirit of many a lad and told her brood:
"If I were you, I would take a leaf out of that new boy's book,"
meaning me!

For a term and a half and not used to such overt affection,
I enjoyed and moped on this kiss of death,
until experience and native cunning told me,
that this wasn't me.
So, studiously, I ignored her attentions,
and refused to join the brood of the weak and unthinking.
But instead, cried like a fountain cascading down the Glens of Antrim,
when a proclamation on the classroom door, declared me, bottom.

That was the first and only time that I was ever bottom of anything,
save in the "mad nun's" book.
There I was either top or bottom, never in the middle,
because, in her pathetic existence, for me,
there was no middle. But,
"What will be will be", and with others I had to endure
mindless pep talks, tolerate her tantrums,
and witness her picking on the weak and making their lives a misery.

As in the early morning darkness, I a prefect,
stood to the side and watched her venom directed at a lad
to whom she had taken an instant dislike.
Raising her hand, just before Mass, and whacking him across the face
she sent his glasses slithering across the polished floor.
And this a school for the blind and partially sighted.

And a friend of mine, with no talent, got a dispensation
and left early for a job in an egg packing station.
While I left on schedule, with no job to go to, despite my industry and thrift
and the fact that I could play, "Sonata in C." by Mozart. But,
"What will be will be", and before we "Irish boys" left, seemingly on mass,
Sister Aloysius had us sitting by the trees, in the spring air, on Sundays,
while she read from "Our Faith."
Conspicuous in her blue serge and white breastplate
and coming, (I think) from Galway; as she read and talked
I sensed that a part of her was leaving
and that she really did care about what might happen to us
in a hostile world.

Principal of the school, she was pragmatic and without vanity.
So when, naively, I told her that I wasn't speaking to the "mad nun"
she didn't say, "How dare you, you insolent boy!"
But contented herself with: "You must always speak with the sisters."

And what of that English Rose, whom all the boys loved,
and whom I loved and feared in equal measure, Sister Clare,
who gave the lie to the cruel jibe that nuns were "jilted women."
Young, vivacious, scholarly and committed, she drove herself to distraction
trying to teach us Latin.
And when she awoke one morning to find she had lost the sight of one eye,
It was as though a sword had pierced all our hearts.
And when, after months of convalescence, she appeared and smiled
And I saw the colour in her cheeks, that hadn't been there before;
I knew how easy it was, for someone, as dynamic and selfless,
to have been neglected.

And Sister Marie.
A country bumpkin from somewhere in Ireland
who had a wonderfully fresh and youthful face,
sparkling eyes, a ready smile, a sense of fun,
and a presence in her posture that was rare.
And who spent her days in boots, in the steam sodden laundry.
And against whom I might have borne a grudge,
for preventing me and a lovely young woman employee
from defining puberty more accurately, but,
that she did it with assurance and grace.

And sister Margaret, retired, and still sacristan.
A gentle woman who wouldn't have said, "boo to a goose."
Who talked fondly of Newry, and probably hadn't been there
for fifty years.

And Reverend Mother, Sister Lucy.
A bulwark of a Lancastrian, who,
arriving after me, was there when I left.
If ever a woman knew how to call a spade a spade

it was Sister Lucy, and she called me "laddie."
And deep in my soul I knew that she was good for the nuns,
and therefore, good for us.
On my way to a party and complaining of a pain in my tummy, she said,
"Ho ho, laddie! You've come to the right place"
and pushed me through the door,
and I never felt better.

And since "What will be will be", and the past is eternally present,
the good, as well as the bad,
I must write about what I know, and in defence of nuns.
And never mind the terrible truth, that I returned home,
a stranger,
and lost,
in my own home town.

My friend and I

My friend and I were meandering home from school
and talking about the teacher, who came from the next big town to us,
when the conversation turned to spelling, and an argument started.
I told him that I knew how to spell ......
the name of the place that our teacher came from.
And he told me, that he too could spell it.
Well, as I did a whirl around a lamp-post
I told him that he couldn't,
and that got his hackles up, and he asked me to spell it.
So quick witted, and logical, and with great authority, I spelled it ......
The name of the place that our teacher came from.
And he told me that I was wrong.
And I told him that I was right.
And he told me that he knew I was wrong,
because his mother had told him how to spell it.
And he too spelled it.
So to make the peace, and as he was coming around to my house,
I told him that I would ask my mother.
And he told me that he was going home to ask his mother.

And I told him that was silly, as my mother was just around the corner.
But turning on his heel he walked back up the hill,
all the way along Main Street, all the way down Causeway Street,
and round to Croc Na Mac.
And I went home and in amazement! told my mother
that even though she was just around the corner
he had gone all that way to ask his mother.
Well, my friend came back round from Croc Na Mac
and all the way up Causeway Street,
(which is a very long street for a small boy),
along Main Street, and down the hill to my house.
And sauntering through the backyard gate,
(with it written down), told me that he was right.
And I told him that I knew he was right,
because my mother had told me, that I was wrong.
Which seemed strange.
Because the name of the place that our teacher came from,
had only two syllables, which was what had made it,
"dead easy" to spell.
Well, the name of the place that our teacher came from
was, COLERAINE, and not COAL RAIN!
And shortly afterwards my friend moved away.
Which was probably just as well.

"I did not say and I would not say"

It was a Holy Year and a good and secure time at home,
with all of us saying the Rosary, and hoping that it was true
that, "the family that pray together, stay together."
And in our house, as in every other house, the prayer ran:
"Enraptured by the splendour of your heavenly beauty,
and compelled by the anxieties of the world..."
Secure, that is, until putting my hand deep into my mother's pocket
I retrieved, not just her rosary, but banknotes, rolled in an elastic band.

It was Saturday, and the mysteries were Glorious!
And like good Catholics we knelt higgledy-piggledy around the room
while our father, in keeping with ancient tradition, mumbled the prayers.
And we got up higgledy-piggledy from our weary knees
to do the things that needed doing, for Sunday Mass.

And having done those things, and having dutifully said, "good night,"
we went to bed, secure from the anxieties of the world,
as we ceased to exist in sleep, as I ceased to exist,
until a distant and wearing voice asked:
"Who delivered the Telegraph?"
"Did you see the boy who delivered it?"
before I was hauled from my bed and downstairs, where,
confused, I knew, that an awesome moment had arrived.
It was not just my father, but he had a curved cane in his hand.

Crying, I told him that I did not steal the money.
And still crying, that I hadn't meant to keep it. So it was easy.
All I had to do was say, why the money was in my pocket.
But I did not say, and I would not say!
So the cane came down without mercy
until the pain was searing through my body
and I was singing and dancing my innocence to heaven,
until reminded, that all I had to do was say,
why the money was in my pocket.

But I did not say and I would not say!
So again, the cane came down without mercy,
until writhing and razed to the ground
and rolling under the table
I turned my face to the wall.

How I got to bed, or how I consoled myself,
or where my mother was, "heaven only knows."
But what I know was the look on her face, when
days later sitting by the fire, and noticing the marks of the beating
still visible on my legs, she said:
"I didn't realise it was that bad."
But no words passed between us.
Because I did not say, and I would not say,
what she must have known.
That I did not say, and I would not say - for her.

A Hard Bargain,

If you are young and say your prayers
before a statue of the Virgin Mary,
pick it up and peep underneath.
For, when I was young, I did,
and found a ten shilling note.
Then curious as a new born lamb
and forgetting my prayers completely,
and dashing into the next room
I turned St. Anthony on his side
and found another ten shilling note.
Then in my excitement and in my pyjamas
and finding no more statues,
I leapt down the stairs wild with excitement
until, hushed, and shushed, and turned around,
I was hurried and scurried up the stairs to bed.
Where, with the door closed,
my old aunt Kathleen told me her secret.

She had a line to Heaven,
to the angels and saints,
to the Virgin and St. Anthony,
and she was driving a bargain.
As soon as they had done
(whatever it was)
that she wanted them to do,
this money would go
to the good causes that she knew
the Virgin and St. Anthony would approve of.
So I went to sleep happy,
knowing that Heaven was a friendly place;
and pleased that I had discovered a grown up's secret.

But when I grew up, I started to worry.

Why were there two lots of money
to different saints
if one saint is as good as another?

And oh dear! was it possible
that my simple old aunt
was not so simple after all,
but making mischief in Heaven,
turning angels and saints
one against the other,
and in the same good cause?

I think not!
Which is why I am telling you,

for I am sure,
that when my old aunt Kathleen
went to Heaven,
she still had secrets,
of her own,
which she packed for the journey.

Grandma

-1-

Do you remember me, Grandma?
You who in your aged blindness
never saw my boyish face,
but knew my voice;
and touching me with your feeble hands,
would marvel at how much I had grown.

-2-

Yes Grandma, I remember you
in all your aged splendour:
especially when standing by your knee
you would draw your black purse
from your black bag, resting on your black apron,
and thoughtfully fondle the coins.

-3-

Do you remember, Grandma,
how polite and studied I was, when,
holding out a coin you would ask:
"How much is that?" And I would tell you?
Well Grandma, it was unbearable!
while you fondled two-and-six.

-4-

Yes Grandma, I remember, how,
when you came to stay,
you would sit to the front in your blindness
taking the sea air
And I especially remember your aloneness
in not being able to see, that beautiful view.

-5-

Do you remember, Grandma,
those long, slow, walks, to the chapel,
when all in black, and resting on my arm,
and supported by your black stick,
I would guide you on and off the pavements
and around the many obstacles until we got there?

-6 -

Yes Grandma, I remember.
And did you ever wonder how, I,
a small boy who liked to leap about the rocks
had the patience for the slow pace?
Or of how others saw me, leading you?
"A case of the blind leading the blind."

-7 -

Do you remember, Grandma,
what we talked about in those timeless moments?
That Grandma, is the one thing I can't remember,
save when by the Salmon Leap you asked to rest.
And I, faced with a choice of three seats asked,
"Which seat would you like to sit on, Grandma?"

-8-

Yes Grandma, I remember
how you laughed and said:
"Why, on my own seat of course."
And how I, sitting beside you, wondered
about Grandmas having a sense of humour,
until it was time to guide you safely home.

-9-

And what Grandma might we have talked about,
had I not been still in my innocence,
but a philosopher seeking out the truth.
Might we have talked about the anvil of life
on which you, Grandma, were forged;
and which left you dignified in old age?

-10-

But, Grandma, it was not decreed
that you and I should exchange such confidences,
but that I should know you only as Grandma,
and be content with that, as you had to be
in not knowing the anvil of life, on which I
like you, would be forged.

-11-
So I remember you, Grandma
frail and vulnerable in your own home;
sitting in the corner by the kitchen fire.
And in your eighties, and in your blindness,
never ever idle, but knitting socks;
and gently pestering them to, "turn the heel."
-12-
Do you remember, Grandma,
the cutlery they brought by the bowl
for you to wash. And the sheets you helped fold.
And how, in the quiet of the afternoon
you would lilt, or sing hymns to Mary,
as mothers sing lullabies to their children?
-13-
Yes Grandma, I remember
the sacredness of that moment,
when, in your frailty, the priest brought Communion.
And of how you would sometimes fret
if Kathleen was too long at the shops.
And of how Kathleen would fret, about you fretting.
-14-
Do you remember Grandma
my taking your picture as you sat
proud and erect in the back parlour;
the last before age took its final toll.
A picture that captured the essence:
Your strength, courage, and alertness?
-15-
I remember Grandma,
because I can see it without looking.
You all in black, with your white hair quaffed
and bedecked with crescent combs.
And those curious black glasses
that far from dimming, gave lustre to your features.

And if I may speak out of turn, Grandma,
and as someone who never heard
a cross word pass your lips;
the lovely thing about that photograph is,
that you are still clutching that black bag,
as it rests, open, on your black apron.

The Vigil

How lopsided and diminished you seemed
sunk there in the armchair,
and perplexing, your grey and balding head, as I,
knowing your intellect, and sitting opposite,
sensed its emptiness, while you, stared and stared,
at nothing in particular.
And how incongruous your impeccable dress,
as waistcoated and in ignorance of me
you raised your glass, studied its impenetrable depth
and gulped it down: gulp, after gulp, after gulp.
"Here's to us! Who's like us?" was what you said,
before again lapsing into muteness.
And how through the evening and long night, hapless,
you shaped my soul. As I, unfeeling, minded you,
and found in the pedimented sideboard,
life! and a crafted beauty! that would endure!
While you, raising your glass yet again, said:
"Up the rebels!" with a vigour that made you sway in your chair,
before looking at me quizzically and asking:
"Am ... I right! or ... am I wrong?"
And I, not knowing who the rebels were, but humouring you said:
"You're right."
"Of course I'm right!" you blathered.
And how unfeeling my handshake, when clasping me,
you, a comrade said;
"put it there, it weighs a tonne!" And asked
with unstoppable drunken mischief:

"What ... weighs ... a tonne?"
How gallant and shrewd my reply.
"I don't know what it is that weighs a tonne,
but whatever it is, it weighs a tonne anyhow."
And how as the evening passed, and the hearth was soiled
with dredged bottles, spittle, and spent matches,
and the air ran pungent with the smell of Stout,
you lapsed, again and again, into unconsciousness;
while I, vigilant, saved all of us
as your cigarette, silent, slipped to the carpet.
But how like a phoenix you rose defiant
and vitriol spewed out.
"Where's your mother?"
"I don't know where she is!"
"I know where she is. The bitch! Oh ho ... I know her form.
She's with Mr. Johnson!"
And how you bastardised all of us, and the song:
""At last, at last, you're in my arms,
you're in my arms where you should be.""
And metamorphosed the question:
"Am I right! or am I wrong?"
"Some people," you said,
"think your old daddy's a fool. But I'm no fool."
Thus reassured, and as a litany,
you denounced each of them in turn
and all of them, (male and female), were, "bitches!
the whole bloody lot of them."
And how against every law,
you raised yourself from your chair,
and swaying through the room
pulled the tablecloth askew as you went,
while I, fearful, sat ready on the edge of my chair.
But how acceptable the sound, knowing that you had been driven
only to urinate in the pantry sink,
while I, scoured the walls and contours of the room
for yet more signs of things durable;
not knowing that you had planted in me,

seeds of a resentment, that years later,
you, for all your powers of intellect, would fail to comprehend,
and about which I would not draw breath to explain.
How I felt the burden of my aloneness,
not knowing where my family were, and certain
that all the world, save you and I were asleep.
And oppressive the darkness through the high window,
as I searched for life; for signs of hope; a greying frown.
Proof, that soon I would be relieved of my burden.
But how like an ox, incredulous you were
when all was lost.
With arm set fair, your grey, spent, head,
studied and studied, and studied, your watch
intent as you still were, on this, elixir of life.
Oblivious you were, of the cold;
of the marble and dead fireplace,
that earlier, in doing what it was supposed to do,
glowed and danced in swirls of gold and purple.
"It's three o'clock," I said, helping the comprehension.
"There's no more drink!
All the bars are closed!
Everyone is in bed asleep!"
"What... time ... is..it?" you drawled,
still bamboozled by your watch.
"It's a quarter past three!"
How especially dreary those moments
as I waited for your will to crumble.
But devious you were to the end.
"Where's ....Deirdre?"
"Deirdre's in bed asleep!"
"Go ... and ... tell her ... I ... want her."
"Deirdre's in bed asleep.
It's very late!
She has to be up for school in the morning!
Everyone is in bed, asleep!"
How remarkable that school of applied psychology, as I,
a mere boy, battered you down with emphasis and repetition.

But more remarkable, nay, miraculous, is the truth,
that despite what had gone before, and would come after,
she, whom you defiled,
would, when the time came,
wail at your passing.

Chain Tig

Let's play Chain Tig! Chain Tig! Chain Tig!
Let's play Chain Tig! "Paddy Joe, you're on!"
"No I'm not! No I'm not!" "Yes you are, Yes you are!"
"No I'm not! No I'm not!" "Yes, yes, you are!"

"Paddy can't catch me, catch me, catch me.
Paddy can't catch me. Paddy Joe is on!"
Paddy comes running, we go running, "Here we are! Where are you?"
"Here I am!" "No you're not. He he he!"

Paddy tags Alice, Alice, Alice.
Paddy tags Alice and she links on.
They come running. We go running. "Here we are! Where are you?"
"Here we are!" "No you're not. He he he!"

The chain's getting longer, longer, longer;
The chain's getting longer and they're after me,
I keep running. They keep after. "Here I am!" Where are they?
"Here we are!" Where am I? Oh dear me!

We run forward, forward, forward.
We run forward and stumble with glee.
The chain pulls this way, the chain pulls that way;
We don't know who we're after so we break in three.

The link can't be broken, broken, broken.
The link can't be broken, so we must agree.
We all run sideways, stretching after Seamus.
And now that he is cornered, we yell with glee.

But Seamus charges at us, at us, at us.
Seamus charges at us, believe you me.
He ducks under arm, and there, trapped, comes to harm.
And Paddy Joe and Alice have the victory.

There's not many left now, left now, left now.
There's not many left now, one, two, three.
The chain pulls this way. The chain pulls that way.
We're chasing after Margaret and we all agree.

She runs this way. She runs that way.
She's getting slower and so are we.
But we pull this way, And we pull that way.
"What?" The bell is ringing. Oh dear me!

Thursday, 9th July 1998

How tranquil the sunset, and gentle the hour,
as we strolled together across the field.
And unplanned, as we descended the lush green slope,
my telling you of my inmost savagery, and you, me,
of your jealousy and possessiveness.
And sensitive and lovely, when passing beneath the trees,
you made room for the infirm: Those men who,
in their frailty, in the twilight, and with their sticks,
struggled to the summit of the gentle slope.
How at peace they seemed, together, and grateful for your kindness.
And what of Jake, who kept us waiting?
I thought of Shelley as you talked, cremated;
and told you of what Scotland meant to me.
You were much too lovely to be "eaten!".
And how appropriate: in those moments, in that place
and at that hour,
that our thoughts were of life - and death.

Friday, 10th July 1998

How you hid your eyes, but not your smile when we met
and I said, "how-ye!"
And you, still smiling, called my name as we passed.

Transcending The Species
For Jenny

IT, stood there;
a space age monument
resplendent in green and white.

A last thought
a parting gift
of the very best.

A testament to love
and tender feeling,
from one mother, for another.

From The Threshold

From the threshold, I had a clear view of the end
of your existence, and can see you now,
pumpkin-faced, smiling, patient and uncomplaining,
but bowed - waiting. Waiting in ease for the sun to set
on that bleak industrial landscape, and rise, flushed in blessing,
when you, in the abundance of your store, would be king.
I had a clear view of your triumph; and can see you now,
cloth cap and blazer, passing contented through the ranks.
Pleased I was, and proud that I had signed the parchment.
But when I signed the parchment to your widow, three weeks later,
and remembered you visiting in your Sunday best, I knew,
that I had been deceived. And that both our stores were empty.

Life

What had he done to raise the hackles of the God who created him?
A model son he was, loved his mother, his country too, for all its
                                                          schizophrenia.
But he died, racked in the rigging of his bed, and wasted to the marrow of
                                                          his bone.
I saw him once: not twice, or three times for the Trinity,
but until the pain in my face was a molecule of the pain in his spine
and I feared, that I might take away his hope.
And what did his mother do, to see her home consumed:
reduced to ash in the white hot heat of bigotry?
And how come she was still standing, listening to me!
                                    to my excuse!
and not spitting venom at the bigots? Those rats,
any one of whom her husband would have saved from drowning,
but that he, "drowned on manoeuvres," while they, choked on their
                                                          xenophobia.
Half slain she was, but she had loved and been loved.
A Boudicca in Belfast, and still nurturing young Lyons.

An Old Song

             Ever present she was
        and the proof was in the singing.
          In her recordings of Jimmy,
             but John, * reincarnated.
         But while Jimmy loved Maureen,
     "The best thing that ever happened to me."
          Maureen feared, "the bottle."
             And going nowhere,
        though Jimmy was always travelling.
          He came to us from nowhere.
            And I went there to stay,
     sleeping with the bare walls and floorboards;
          and to the sound of Maureen
          sobbing alone in the darkness.
       "Don't worry", she said in the light,
        "it's only because of the baby."

34

The new one, which she took
along with the other one to her mother.
                    *

It wasn't long before the neighbour
      noticing that I was on my own
sent her daughter in to keep me company.
What an occasion of sin, that might have been
but that I didn't mind being alone, until
                  startled!
            by the kerfuffle.
            It was Jimmy
He had gone to work in the darkness,
            and in the darkness
and in the confused state of his brain,
      could not quite make it home.
                    *

I could smell the cooking when I got in.
It was unbelievable. Maureen was back
      and in the kitchen, and in a temper.
She had found my dinner and binned it.
"IT ISN'T FIT FOR A DOG TO EAT!"
                    *

      I don't know if he, Jimmy
      was caught in that whirlwind,
and didn't ask when I saw him last.
      A dapper wee man
breezing through the centre of Belfast.
Everything in his garden was lovely;
      and he was still travelling.
                    *

            "I'm starting a new job
                  on Monday."

* The Irish tenor, John McCormack

The End

It came in the loneliness of night
with no one attending our needs,
save a nurse who came and went discretely.
Illumined he was in his cot by the hovering wall-light;
while his sister, in her simplicity and ignorance,
hailed "the death rattle," and his brother,
a saint in his own right, organised the prayers.
In pairs, and on either side, and on our knees,
we interceded, until the Almighty laid claim to his soul;
and his helpmate, whose very essence was being ripped apart,
cried to Heaven.

Landscapes

Who knows what anguish was laid to rest,
or sense of failure and shame was stilled,
when the priest commended his soul to God,
and his body, wasted, to the ground.

More searing then than death, was life,
was youth, on that deciduous landscape,
where, gnawed by falsehood and by truth,
I scoured them, "mourners" in frosted light.

Black shadows they were, in that Apocalypse.
Deceivers, whose truth I sought to reconcile to my truth.
And what of her truth? She who,
numbed by suffering, was pivotal to all of us.

Monumental then, it was: the life wasted,
the lives blighted, the resentments suppressed;
and profound the truth: that I did not love, and had never loved,
he, who had joined the Communion of Saints.

The Victory

On his knees he cried:
"We've won! We've won!"
before madly leaping about the room.
Oblivious he was,
to the wear and tear on the carpet
and the certainty, (or so it seemed),
that the settee would be ground to a pulp,
until the phone rang. Then changing tack
he leapt and danced across the hall, and back,
flushed and choking on his words.
And when it rang again, it was his mum again.
So I like Bayern, was there - just.
Which was why I didn't say,
it's only a game, or as nothing
compared to the suffering in Kosovo.
But with reverence:
"Shall we go to Manchester?"

Rearing up, and Schmeichel like, he lunged, screaming:
"I love you! I love you! I love you!"
And hugged me like I was the European Cup.

The Homecoming

As nothing now they were
those great imponderables,
those mysteries of life,
that bent the minds of Plato and Aristotle,
and sent believers wantonly to run against the Turks.
As nothing, now that the Huns lay prostrate
before the Gods at Nou,
and Mecca was in Manchester.

Insight

What else could you possibly want to be
but a mariner. Yet, they just couldn't see it.
"Is there a sea-faring tradition in the family?"
they asked, perplexed. And she said, "no", perplexed.
And the window was open and the sun was shining.
And the blue lagoon that was the Atlantic, was a playful place.
And beyond the lagoon the golden sand gleamed in the sunlight.
Yet they still couldn't see it!
For they had lived their lives in offices,
and filled their heads with theories
and were bamboozled -
by white linen tablecloths and silver condiment sets.

These were good people, who had my interests at heart.
But they just couldn't see it.

Brothers and Sisters

Strangers we were to one another
As we went about our separate lives
But shoring up the edifice,

For there was a life still standing,
Fragments, from what might have been,
But that she was exhausted.

For the mouths of her babes and sucklings
Had been stopped; and their beating hearts subdued,
And their souls made adult before their time.

So there was then, no uproarious laughter.
No sharing of hopes and fears.
And no excited, whispered, teenage revelations.

Just a life that should have been.
A shimmering translucent beauty
Eclipsed, by a grey and mizzled dawn.

The Generation Gap

His world is an armchair
or a beanbag wrapped in a football logo;
or a console on which he tests
his brain, his precision and skill.
A static spot in which the adrenalin flows
as he pumps and pumps the console
until his brain and his reflexes are in trim.

But what if the boat were sinking,
or an Arctic Winter came again,
Or he was trapped on a cliff face.
Would he have the staying power
and the presence of mind to construct a survival plan?

Through the wild grass we ran,
Indians in the hills.
And as commandos, parachuted
from the promenade to the distant sand below.
Over boulders we clambered,
and steadied our gait on slimy surfaces
And seeing and feeling the ravages of nature
learned to be fearless and know that you could survive.
And pell-mell we extended our legs
in pursuit of tyres rolling downhill,
and bicycled hands free!
and swam before breakfast and before bed.

Make no mistake. He's my son and I love him.
But we were a part of nature.
And our bodies and our minds were trim.
Because we, played on the earth.

Genesis

Instinctively, I studied it:
a grey, heaving, frothing, undulating mass,
and tuned my ear to the wind
as it swept in gusts around the windows
and like a Banshee whined beneath the door.

Safe and squat, I studied it:
the dull thud, and the blast!
and the shapes distended, dissipating in the wind;
and cast my eye to the Skerries, black and agitated,
and to the coaster, perilous in their lee,
appearing, disappearing, and reappearing.

And through the darkness, I studied it;
that relentless, mindless roar;
and as a lookout, I was there in the morning light;
to witness that rage, still white and unabated;
and the coaster,
defiant!
appearing, disappearing and reappearing.

And as the waves stretched their writhing tentacles,
and pounded towards the nucleus of my being;
I watched,
and wondered.
Unwitting.

The Lifeboat

When the dull thud of the maroon
burst above the town,
every pulse quickened
and sense was magnified,
as the implosion displaced the core of being.
And every ear suspended,
waited in trepidation,
for a sound unfailing.
A second dull thud above the town.

A special sound.
Our sound.
Not heard in towns inland,
nor in the country,
but our unique cry for help.

An essence of being
where men
unknown and unseen
abandoning normal things,
veered out into the abyss.

Their testament?
An omni-presence

A gravitation that drew me
fearless, fighting, and in pursuit,
out against the wind
along the narrow abandoned streets
down on to the harbour
where, ignoring things secure
and battling right out to its mouth
and clambering to the sea wall,
I raised *my prow* to the wind.
To elements raw and unrestrained
that in an instant
chilled to the marrow of my bone

and forced me!
back down to the harbour.

And there it was,
where it had always been,
silent, and stable on its stilts.
And as I contemplated
that moment,
frozen in time -
the doors flung wide! above the slipway;
I knew what courage was;
and that I,
lived in a great place.

Foyle St. (1)

Sinister it was, with its windows black and barred
gawping at me from across the street.
Relentless as it consumed its prey
protesting, as it slithered into the arched mouth.

Intense the mingling and numerous the shapes
that passed in that narrow confine;
where man and beast, outsider and insider
jostled for their rightful place.

Cars, and the Red Hand of Ulster.
Hooves, in dry laboured clatter.
Pigs pleading. Hay akimbo.
And the wide eyes of Cantrell & Cochrane.
And the sleek electric bread- van.
Barrels: refined shapes, layer on layer passing.
People. And the skittish horse;
its cartwheels twisting like windmills.
Space - Silence - Fear
and
Defiance!

Foyle St. (2)

Grey and drab it was in the evening
when the rhythm of work and men had ceased
save for the lights -

Stop!
Get ready!
Go!

And the hoardings proclaiming to no one.
And when the sky was black,
the orange lamps lighted,
and the street and the mill-face ghastly,
it was time for bed,
for the orange glow through the blinds,
and the light, elongated,
that sometimes, passed across the ceiling.

Christmas Shopping

I saw a card in a shop today,
it almost frightened my brain away.
Like a dirty mag I put it back,
but retrieved it again from among the pack.
And there it was for all to see,
the changing face of the family tree.
And now that my life is near its end,
the greeting was: "To Mum and friend."

Christmas

There were no rocket boosters then, to confound the night sky,
just unsubtle floodlights, hauled out and in place for the occasion,
their gentle beams firing the majestic spires
and dissipating in the gloom.

And no exotic digital displays, nor laser lights,
but an innovation: a speaker above the hardware store,
from which Bing, to a dark and near deserted street, crooned;
and only Rudolph ran strictly to tempo.

But a time it was, of innocence and quiet excitement,
when the air was as pure and life as certain
as the cotton wool on the crib was white.
And when every rooftop and every chimney, unencumbered
were objects of wonder.
And the black laneway - a sanctuary.
And sleep - a nuisance.
And socks hanging in a drab kitchen -
an adventure.
When "Postman's Knock", "Forfeits", and "The Queen of Sheba"
brought joyous laughter.
And voices: adult voices, modulated,
blended with play,
and the texture and fragrance of marzipan.

Remembering

I did not want to be among the remembering,
nor walk the black macadam out of duty,
nor intone any note of tenderness or of compassion,
but instead, to make my way against the chill wind of truth.

So alone I walked to piping Oystecatchers
and gazed incredulous at the deceit, hot springs
rising in stealth from an Arctic Sea, until they, and I
resolutely ascending and rounding the headland,
were subsumed in liquid flint.

Gone now, were the rugged contours, the purple hills,
the golden dunes and defiant basalt causeway.
But this: dank, cold, and disfigured, was our world.

For she was strong and he was weak.
She provided and he squandered.
But when the anchor failed,
and an anchor must not fail!

Cast off, she was, for the rock of self reliance.

I did not want to be among the remembering,
nor walk the black macadam out of duty,
nor intone any note of tenderness or of compassion,
but instead, to make my way, *remembering,*
against the chill wind of truth.

"Lodged in the caverns of my being"

Lodged in the caverns of my being,
were silences, glimpses of burdened souls,
and echoes of a pensive secret self.
Stirrings. unsought pointers to despair.

I found them, words of gentleness and love
hewn from knowledge and experience.
Her secret seeking out. Priestly council:
"A Few Words of Encouragement."

And a replica: cold steel
in an undignified dishevelled bed.
His secret; an asking for forgiveness.
Christ crucified: a refuge in the night.

School

To the memory of Master Fitzpatrick
for whom I have always had a soft spot.
Notwithstanding his faults, in my case,
he was inspirational

———————

It was always there.
Its broad sloping slated roof
and gable chimneys,
solemn and erect against the sky.
Unyielding.
Unfeeling of my need to know,
save that in time, I too.
skewered from my path,
would be dragged between the railing and high stone wall,
down into its innermost depth.

"Who struck McCormack?" *
"The man with the caster hat!"
A morning ritual on the way to school,

46

as mysterious as the solitary gull
fretting above the rooftops.
Or the morning papers, bundled and abandoned in the doorway.
A slow place
where rock-faced cladding, spires and lawns,
bristled in clean air.

They took a battering ram to my consciousness:
a work of genius.
Cost?
A penny!   *
I loved the feel of it,
and the smell of it when it was new;
and its small pages, crammed with the printed word.
A masterpiece!
A literary gem of rhyme and repetition.
A book in which big words were linked to big ideas.
And where "nothing" no longer meant nothing,
but something,
because we were made from nothing.
A world in which anything was possible,
because nothing was impossible.
And three in to one did go!   *
And where there was no need to worry
about not knowing the answer,
because some questions
HAD NO ANSWER.
And besides,
this world was not the real world,
because there was a world elsewhere.

So I wondered.
And raising my eyes to the high gable window
BELIEVED!
that if you could get a window that high up
anything was possible.

So blithely we skipped
through this Holy Spirit world
of:
Creation
Incarnation
and Redemption.
Resurrection
and Ascension.
Heaven
and Hell.
Sacraments
and Sacramentals,
Sacrilege
and Sin.
Mortal Sin
and Venial Sin.
And Perfect
and Imperfect
Contrition.
Confession
and Absolution.
Confirmation
and Transubstantiation.
Of
heretics,
infidels,
Indulgences and
TRUTH!

I did not hear the subtle roar of dogma,
as I watched the waves, white on a silver sea
rasp and rise towards the shore.
But I saw the grains of sand passing in shadows
and the dunes with their scrawny heads.
I was a schoolboy musing -
This was how it had always been.

And this was a moment of truth
bereft of bravado.
We were solemn and listening
and he was flexing it.
"This," he said, "is the Black Doctor
I prescribe the dose, and the Doctor gives it!"

But he taught in fits and starts.
And disappeared in fits and starts.
So we outmanoeuvred him in fits and starts.
And with the room in uproar,
cribbed the answers from his book.
And while he brewed his tea on the hearth
and communed with the Devil in Hell;
in stealth - I rose from my chair
and poked my toe at his bum.

"Beyond the East!" I told them pointing
"the sunrise!
Beyond the West, the sea.
And East and West" I told them flailing,
a wander thirst, that will not let me be."

My Sunflower Girl

I will hear your voice in bird song,
and find your love in sunlight and dappled shade,
and your gifts, in the colour and fragrance of flowers.
And I will cry with you in the rain.
For my path will be your path, and my breath your breath.
And you will be there in the moonlight and in the stars.
And your warmth will reach me, even on frosted ground.
For the willow will be revived.
And the birds will soar and sing.
And in the breeze, I will whisper - "Hello!"
And as you turn to the sun, I will turn to you.
My Sunflower Girl.

Daddy

A cultured man, a refined man, who,
from the pages of legend, gave me my name.

A silent man, a violent man, who,
in his addictions, stifled, hope and love.

An inadequate man, a moral man, who,
in his floundering, squandered pity.

Messing It Up

Life would not be life, if it was satisfactory;
which is why we live on the edge of an abyss,
waiting for the moment when we mess it up completely.
And life would not be life, without the will to cling on -
at least until tomorrow,
so that we can marvel at yesterday,
and wonder about today,
and look forward to tomorrow, knowing -
that that, just might be the day, when we will -
mess it up - completely.

For The Young

Shut down the television, close down the internet,
save them from the cut-throat glare.
Young minds, young hearts, nurtured in twilight hours.
Let mongrels bark, birds sing, and mute fish swim;
and don't explain why they, and you are here.
But hark! I hear a baby crying in the reeds;
and straining hearts calling a mellow tune.
For hope has stirred! And sunlight spoiled the night!
And the Pied Piper is calling a different tune.
And the gangly sunflower: still doing what sunflower's do,
has turned its back on the harbinger of death.

Liberation

I think he's dead.
I think they're dead too.
But they live on together;
He and they - a gracious gentle people.
Crucified; he stole a glance and saw them
crying, and to order
baying for his execution -
Their "Spiritual Father."

An Invitation Upon Retirement

Hello, my good people, wherever you are.
That old bastard Cormac is travelling far.
Like a fox he is leaping right out of his lair
and heading for freedom, shouting, "come if you dare!"
down to the Rushcutters where the swans gently swim
and crowd round the bar where we'll make a wild din.
There with hand in his pocket and full of good cheer,
he will buy you a Guinness, Schnapps cocktail or beer.
And tell you it's heaven to be warm here within;
a fine recompense for a lifetime of sin.
And he'll offer a few words of thanks to you all
for shared times in the trenches, where the shrapnel did fall.
And we'll toast our great leaders with their backs to the wall.
And from under their "vision" to freedom we'll crawl.
So leave your "compooters" and stats on the wall.
And allow me to thank you. I love you all.

Marking Time
For Jenny

"How long have you to go now?"
"Eight weeks."

"Hi! I suspect you're counting the days?"
"Four weeks and three and a half days," I said
trying to hide my feeling of satisfaction.

"Not long now?"
What day is it?...Friday? Ah yes! Two weeks today."

I must start to think ahead, plan my day.
No need to get up at five, eight will do.

You must get in to the habit of reading contemporary writers.
And brush up on current affairs.
And get the Sunday papers, and make them last the week.
And think about joining a writing group.
And get back into singing at folk clubs.

I could feel her hands on my back, warm and reassuring
as I wept.
I had tried to be matter of fact.
But I was off to the chest pain clinic in the morning.
And there were just twelve days to go.

Before Time

I was there before the dawn of time
when man was given his state of consciousness
and the umbilical cord was first let loose upon the elements.
When there were no constraints, no moral imperatives,
and Christ had not been crucified.

I was taken there while my soul was in formation,
back to where the elements raw and unrestrained
washed over me in waves of being.
Disfigured: I have returned to that raw hallowed place,
to be refreshed, and give thanks.

Sinister Forces

They were running full throttle in the name of liberation
and lighting our darkness with a cacophony of sound;
while their souls, believing, were long gone from their sacrificial offerings.

They were liberating me, though I was drinking in a beer-keller:
shutting out the obscenity: clinging to life.
"It's OK", I said. "He's with us, we'll get him home."

Swift as the night owl they had us in their talons.
Mercifully, and out of sight, they wanted him for a quiet word,
while leaving me to contemplate their metallic limbs - spreadeagled.

As if from nowhere, they appeared in the doorway, wise men from the East
eye-balling, and wanting to know what the no good pigs were up to.
It was my soul they were after, and all I had to do was get stuck in.

"I'm a doctor", he said, ignoring my gospel of peace.
"You may be a doctor, but that doesn't make you God!"
In the darkness, this new gospel made his friend nervous.

Italy 2006
For Brendan on his 60th birthday

Venice
Out of the darkness, light. Pentecost.
Tongues of painstaking fire.
More telling than the "big bang"
and the complex world in which we live.
Beauty in bronze. Still life
unfazed by time and the rising tide.
Balm for the soul.

Florence
I wouldn't want to live there.
It felt like indigestion.
Too much beauty in too small a space;
and the multitude, not knowing which way to turn.
Thank God for the Ponte Vecchio, San Marco, and Fra Angellico.
For light, air, commerce, and a quiet devotion
to faith and love.
And for the cash machine, that at intervals
brought manna from England.

Sienna
What a scandal it must have been
those Dominicans fighting over her,
so that her head is in one place
and her torso in another.
Objects of veneration. An affront to decency.
And what a shame that her kitchen and bedroom are frescoed.
Much better to see pots and pans and know that they were hers.
But her spirit lives in the durable.
In the muted tints that spring into life in the sunshine.
And in the cathedral, whose inner beauty
surpasses that of Florence.

Rome
I've gone off Italian women, young and middle aged
who got up to give me their seat.
I'm only sixty-four.
And I have harsh words for the Sistine Chapel:
Overrated, overstuffed. and at twelve Euros.
And for the vain and foolish ushers, clapping their hands
and shushing the multitude, who unsuspecting, take up the call.
There are stunningly beautiful temples in the suburbs.
Someone said, that Christ is disproportionate to the rest of the Pieta.
Strange. I always thought that Mary's shoulders were too broad.
A masterpiece!
Perhaps on "the last day" the Almighty will give it the final touch:
Arteries.

St. Peter's Square

It is a truly spectacular arena, St. Peter's Square:
In bright sunlight, with the choir singing, the faithful at prayer,
and the Cardinal's impeccable decibels reaching above and beyond
the work of Bernini.
Strange, how the tourists can chatter, seemingly unmoved.
And the Romans, let the occasion pass them by.
But an inner voice is speaking,
reminding me not to confuse faith with spectacle.
And I am reminded of Mother Theresa, who,
stayed, for just as long as it took to greet,
her friend, and spiritual father.
A colossus - in the arena of life.

Conscience

I am troubled by begging and struck by the fact that,
in England, there are good days and bad days for doing it.
And I am disturbed by my distrust of the poor.
But it is different in Italy.
There they sit on the pavement with their pathetic cup,
and face buried, because "begging is shameful."
Or smartly dressed, accost you with their baby on the station concourse,
and challenge you with the sign of the cross.
And I am disturbed by my distrust of the poor.
To Christ, I turn for solace. Didn't he say:
"The poor will always be with you,"
when his disciples were indignant at the cost of the ointment.
He must understand? There has to be room for manoeuvre?
Here, we are arguing about the veil.
In the Medina there was no argument.
Veiled, she came after my hand, kissing it.
And I had given a pittance.

A Poem for My 65th Birthday

Happy Birthday
A Philosophical Treatise

I'm sixty five today.
And do you know what the nicest thing about it is?
I have my whole life in front of me.

The Ulster Crow

The throttle was the signal it was time to say goodbye
To "the mountains and the gantries" and McCooey's.
And the chimneys crowded in as we veered across the line
Rat-a-tat-tat, rat-a-tat-tat- to Antrim.
"Up the airy mountain and down the rushy glen,"
A matchbox of a station and no wee men.
And rat-a-tat-tat, rat-a-tat-tat, out along the line, to Ballymena.
No sign of St. Patrick, or pilgrims from the hill,
Just the dry growl of diesel and red brick chill.
And the full-time whistle that sent us on our way,
Past ruminating Friesians and steers coloured honey
North to Cullybackey and the townland of Money.
But Coleraine was where the action was, a regular little hive,
With its spiky little fascias, and factual Ulster tones:
"Change here for Portstewart and Portrush!"
And iron wheeled trolleys sleeping on the cobbles.
Out we'd go between the gates, the traffic standing still,
Rat-a-tat-tat, rat-a tat-tat, over the bridge, over the Bann
And we'd peep out the window looking for the thrill,
Looming ever larger, Downhill.
Rat-a-tat-tat in the darkness. Rat-a-tat-tat in the light
Rat-a-tat-tat in the darkness, and out into the light
Of the brash rolling Atlantic and cabins tumbling: Downhill.
And lifeless Castlerock and Bellarena.
Then rat-a-tat-tat, rat-a-tat-tat, south-west across the plain.
And straight across the runway in our clapped out train.
Then cranking along the river bank, the maiden hills in view.
Past where St. Columba left a footprint with his shoe.
We edged along the Waterside, the lie less than true.
But with the "oak grove" near, we were free from fear -
And hours of boredom.

The Red Hand Of Ulster

It's stuck fast to my consciousness and I miss it
like the little black fellow on the marmalade.
It didn't hurt me in any way, and was
about as bigoted as my grandmother's drawing-room clock.
The worst that it could do was cover its face with its hands.
And it couldn't keep a secret.
And sad to say, it has been laid to rest in landfill Norfolk.

Though a wordsmith, I am in awe of the visual image
whose power, in an instant, is vast and indecipherable.
And of the Red Hand, that never held a Kalashnikov
nor threw a petrol bomb. And that with impunity
got about on public transport.

The stuff of legend, it is almost, but not quite defunct.
And who would have thought that I would come to prefer it
to the insipid shamrock.

St. Alexis
Good Friday 1961

Innocent, they frolicked about the lawn
and I didn't think to ask: "Who made thee?"   *
Or fret, when in cassocks and black as crows
they gathered to say goodbye.
Looking them in the eye, I took my leave
and left them - to meditate:
on faith, justice, and wrong doing.

The Portrait

It caused consternation but the dye was cast.
And I was too dismayed to know how to explain.
And I can't be sure why I choose
The colour purple.
Was it innate wisdom? A case of
"Out of the darkness, light."
They say that purple denotes "royalty" and "wealth"
"Wisdom and spirituality". I like the sound of that.
Much better than "exotic" or, "artificial".
But whatever else, it is unmistakably me!
Not us! But three score years of me
Full bodied and smiling.
And they are in the substance.

Building Walls

A public spirited neighbour, called to break the news.
Through the latticed windows I was suspicious
And she was apologetic.
Together we went to take a look, and there it was;
The handy work of mindless morons, strewn
Across the pavement and into the road.
No one, seeing what had happened, called to raise the alarm.
For hours, they stepped over it, walked around it,
Or drove past. And this a village community.
There's no "knife crime" here - not yet.
Mercifully, just bricks, fragments of disordered minds.

A Poem for My 66th Birthday

Fatigued by the writings of Sylvia
I turned to the window, and fog.
And despairing and lost, Beyond Kinsale,
I fragmented the Grecian Urn.
And Robert Frost has taught me a lesson:
That the last thought belongs to "me"!
And the doctor's receptionist knows,
That that nice old man has lost his marbles.
But as men find God, I have found Tulips.
And to you my Alma Mater:
"When I have fears that I may cease to be,"
Bugger off! I'll live FOREVER!

"In the long ago"

I was a man of principle in those days, hardly out of nappies,
and keen on future happiness,

though the prospects were bleak as I swung the lead weights
of the bench hand-press.

But good souls made it bearable. And I had a stab at
the nine First Fridays.

And prayed when no one suspected, and kept my priorities
in good order.

On the rare occasion that I approached the Machine Shop late,
it was always on a full stomach.

And I was wiser than the wisdom of old men, and women, who,
confided in me as you would a guru.

And patient, as they unburdened their uncertain souls.
Sadnesses that are with me still.

As is cantankerous Bob. Gentle Ivor, Jean in her sinful softness.
Sadie: "good living", and Hannah.

And Jimmy: coarse and as complex as an old rope.
And Dorothy: rouged and knowing.

And bigotry among those not long out of nappies, I challenged
head on, so that she,

the Virgin Mary reappeared in my room. And the miracle?
My not needing to know the culprit.

Walking through the packed church, I was late,
but before the high altar, the coffin was patient.

It was the 5th of February and the last in a rerun
of the nine First Friday's.

And time

for Requiem Mass for my father.

And the tide was turning.

Friendship
For Arthur and Elizabeth Campbell

I want you to be remembered down the ages.
Pure goodness and dry wit combined.

In those troubled times you emerged - insignificant;
and told me of your intriguing past;
and guided me through the heartland of murderous loyalism
to meet Elizabeth.

Arthur and Elizabeth.

Who had the audacity
to call you Arthur?

Ah! The penny has dropped! Of course! Arthur Guinness!
Nothing to do with the round table.
Your father was a lover of the black stuff.
And the minister can't have asked what he was up to.

Saint Arthur?

But Elizabeth was what an Elizabeth should be:
"Gracious", shapely and good.
It can't have been your looks she was after, but the heart.

How did you, Elizabeth, do it?
Nurse the sick, raise your brood, and keep him on his feet
while he poked around in filing cabinets,
Worried
Philosophised
And smoked through his coal scoured bronchial tubes.
And miraculously, sang in the choir.

Soon we will be gone, as will be the memories, as is Maura.
Do you remember how, on Ramore Head
We bathed in freedom
And the view.

Trapped

It might have been a doll's house, set apart as it was on a drab street
Double-fronted, and with roses peeping through the railings.
Its prosperous aspect, perplexing my eye as I passed.

Delighted she was that I was coming to stay. A room to the front
With two singles and a double all to myself.
And with the Virgin Mary having pride of place on the mantelpiece.

I had just set foot through the door when I was cornered in the hall.
She must have seen me coming down the drab street.
She was up to "high doh" and wanted me to know that Jose was only "a halfer"

I hadn't heard the expression before, but the Holy Spirit was hovering
For I knew what she meant. But again,
When she cornered me in the hall to talk about Arthur

The Holy Spirit was not so helpful, because she had it on the highest authority:
From England! that should he convert, and marry Jose - who was only "a halfer",
He would loose his inheritance.

Brian, a protestant, who could keep his own council, was courting and
Taking instruction. While home for the weekend she would ponder
the question. Will he? Won't he? And with me cornered in the hall.

She never ever cornered me in the hall to talk about the other Brian
Who lived at the head of the stairs: educated, sarcastic, and a bigot,
Not from Protestant Ulster, but from Dundalk.

But she cornered me in the hall to talk of her relief at finding
Not one, but two Catholics to share my room.
And I knew that the Virgin Mary had something to do with it.

I had just set foot through the door when she cornered me in the hall.
We were back in the 30s, in Dublin for the Eucharistic Congress.
She had followed it on "Radio Eireann", and had fallen in love with the hymn:
"Faith of Our Fathers". And it could have been yesterday.

The Blackbird

My little friend he sits and sings
cocooned within his shapely wings.
As black as night, as brash as day
he lifts his head and sings away,
and looks askance when I appear
and with my camera interfere.
He seems so puny here below
from where I watch the fishes go.
And sings the harder round about,
as patient, by the water spout
I watch the silver liquid flow
then awkward, round the garden go.
A little here, a little there,
while he calls out his evening prayer;
and warns the fellows round about
that he'll defend this garden stout.
The snails, the worms, oh so slow
are for his wife, he'll have them know.
Then from the ridge he takes to flight
and on a wired pole alights
and sings a while before he goes
to where the twisted willow grows.
The boundaries he is making clear:
There is no Bed & Breakfast here!
Then back upon the rooftop he,
looks yet again askance at me.
For I am feeling humble now,
and watching, while he takes a bow.
And waiting, for the sunset low
on his extended chest, to show.

For Deirdre on Her Birthday

Well, look at it this way Deirdre, you could be dead.
And you can toast your toes on all those candles.
And in no time at all you'll be a granny.
Granny Deirdre!

"This little ... cow, went to market. This little cow..."

"Eene meeny mine mo, catch the ... the ... kitten! by the toe."

"Cuchi, cuchi, cuchi coo!"

A Poem for My 67th Birthday

Why?

He is thirty-seven and has gone to prison for two years.
Hopefully his wife and three children will wait.
Solomon - in all his wisdom would have sent him home
to grieve: for Willow, Angel, Thor and Keavy.
Every day he will feel a failure.
Every time he sits down to eat he will see their young faces
and loathe the spare cash.
And forgiveness will not erase
the stamp - the indelible mark on his soul.

Lough Derg

I went there for my sins, twice,
and was a hero before leaving home.
Even Molly, my landlady, wearied from toil,
and fearing that my strength might fail,
cooked a huge fry forenenst midnight,
then left me alone to eat it.

And a girl, a pilgrim, keeling over,
slept on my shoulder to Pettigo,
where quietly herded into broad-beamed boats
and set strangely low in the water,
we ploughed our way across the swell
the ripples shaded, spouting as they passed,
like wearied souls, warning of our fate
on that Purgatory of stone.

Registered, fasting and barefoot,
we hobbled across the slivers of stone
to that living tomb, St. Patrick's Basilica,
from whence a steady stream of living souls,
coming - were going to St. Brigid's Cross,
where, with arms abashed, they renounced
the devil, his works, and his pomps, as prelude
to an orgy of prayer and carnal pain
around the penitential beds.
Those circular walls set in jagged rock,
around which, before which, and within which
Paters Aves and Creeds subdued the flesh.
And where the pilgrim with faltering gait, welcomed
the silent guardian with outstretched hand.
Then, footsore by the water's edge,
more Paters, more Aves and a Creed,
Before dancing across those slivers of stone,
back to that whited sepulchre to pray,
Paters and Aves for the Pope's intentions.

And all this while, the repentant soul
fevered in knowing of the deadline,
for wads of bread and black tea.

Then as respite from *unfamiliar* penance,
and as assurance and fortification for the vigil:
(that penitential period of absence from sleep),
a feast! of varied and familiar devotions,

before that drab basilica echoed and re-echoed
to voices in unison proclaiming:
"Our Father, who art in Heaven...".
And flatly: "Hail Mary full of grace...",
while still in our bared feet.
And with the oppressive blackness of night
pressing in through the high sanctuary windows,
we walked the isles and as instructed,
stood and knelt, enacting the penitential beds.
At 12:15 am, the fourth Station commenced.
More Pater Nosters, more Aves and a Creed.
At 1:45 am, the fifth Station commenced.
More Pater Nosters, more Aves and a Creed.
At 3:15 am, the sixth Station commenced.
More Pater Noster's, more Ave's and a Creed.
At 5:00 am, the seventh Station commenced.
More Pater Nosters, more Aves and a Creed.
And between each Station, homilies,
from seemingly dreary, and seemingly vain pilgrim priests;
until hope, in daylight and fresh air
began to permeate through the basilica doors.
And longing - to be embraced by nature's light,
and drink the draught of nature's space;
and see heron skimming across the Lough,
before morning prayer, Mass, instruction,
and the blessing of pious objects.

And now embarked on the second day
with confession and the ninth station completed,
and mindful of the adage old:
"that the devil makes work for idle hands,"
the penance now was to stay awake,
while subduing the pangs of hunger,
for wads of bread and black tea.
So noticing the timelessness of the Lough,
and sensing the oppressiveness of the place,
we drew strength in the certain knowledge

that we were not in that boat
of new pilgrims arrived at the jetty.
Or in that new and patient queue
of young and old in their rainwear,
for the first of the penitential beds.
And we noted with envy, the priest,
who, in his cassock and in his shoes,
and eagle-eyed, scrutinised the young
for the slightest hint of unbecoming character.

And I, for my part, as recommended,
sought inspiration among the hospice sages.
Men of the sod who herded together
around the vat of Lough Derg soup.
Old weather-beaten and young robust men.
Legendary masters in the art of conversation,
to whom I listened intently, and more intently,
as their babble rebounded on raw stone;
before quietly withdrawing, amazed -
Uncomprehending of brogues from as far South
as mine was from the far North.

And stark on the morning of the third day
the call to prayer and final repentance:
Paters and Aves by St. Patrick's Cross.
And the devil renounced with arms aloft.
Then four times round that whited sepulchre
to seven decades of the Holy Rosary.
Then back across those slivers of stone
to the circular walls set in jagged rock,
around which, before which, and within which,
Paters. Aves and Creeds subdued the flesh;
and where the pilgrim, with faltering gait
welcomed the silent guardian with outstretched hand.
Then barefoot by the water's edge,
final Paters, and final Aves, and a Creed
before returning to that living tomb to pray,

Paters and Aves for the Pope's intentions.

And when in the luxuriance of our shoes
we averted the eyes of the disembarked,
our faith was in the power of the drover.
High, and silent above the stern,
rhythmically he eased us out into the Lough.
Stroke, by stroke, by stroke,
he was returning us from whence we had come:
to the crucible - to life.

Making Mischief
   for Vijay

The Liverpool Manager, Rafa,
Committed a bit of a gafa,
He jumped up and down, and then he did frown
And got on the phone to Sir. Alex.

"The trouble with you is you like a good stew:
Too many onions and fritters;
They're left on the bench and create such a stench,
That the Kop it is riddled with jitters.

"Now you know my old friend Arsene Wenger,
Or that goofy-looking fellow from Ulster,
They're better than you, for like me, they knew,
That the Season began in September.

"As downward you go, you put up a good show
Of declaring an upward intention,
But according to Moyes, your collection of boys
Are seriously lacking invention.

"So what can I do that I might help you,
The referees know I am willing.
Shall I read out a note having first cleared my throat,
As you know the result can be thrilling.

"No! Here's what I'll do, that I might help you,
Next time you come to Old Trafford......
What! Lend you Tevez? Sacre bleu!
Sorry Rafa, wrong language......
Should auld acquaintance be forgot?
Aye - and never! called t' mind."

An Antique Christmas

Cormac:
"I'll pay by MasterCard from the UK
And I would like it in time for Christmas."

Dianne:
"I'm so sorry Cormac, it was sold last week."

Cormac:
"How about GL108 or GL106?"

Dianne:
"The green and clear jug is nice;
The basket is nice too, but I prefer the jug.
The basket I will dig out
As it will be packed down somewhere.
Have a think and let me know."

Cormac:
"It sounds as though you enjoy your job;
And the offer of a discount is much appreciated.
The add says that the jug, "is crying out for flowers,"
But the basket, (to me), seems the most suitable.
But whichever you decide, I will have."

Dianne:
"Cormac, I searched high and low but failed to find the basket.
It isn't where it's supposed to be.
I'll look again on Saturday.
PS. The glass jug is here I have that."

Cormac:
"I think my preference is for the basket.
It is more unusual than the jug
But if you can't turn it up tomorrow, I'll settle for the jug.
Your website should carry a health warning: lots of lovely stuff there."

Dianne:
"Cormac, apologies for the delay in answering,
Only the basket wasn't found until 5 pm this evening.
TRUE! It is delightful, nicer than the jug.
It is hand blown by Murano. Your wife will love it!"

Cormac:
"You're an angel! (From a distance at least.)"

A Poem For My 68th Birthday

He called it many things, the hand of time;
A "bloody tyrant" reaping with its scythe.
And like the hawks that circled overhead
Laid claim to life, even if he were dead.
    And I have measured it, that self same hand:
In life, in epitaph and infant death;
And thinking on what was and might have been,
Have marvelled that I should be here at all.
    But now my body, slavish, lags behind;
The tigerish sinews they are wearing thin.
And still I boast that I am well preserved;
And overlook the medical hors-d'oeuvre.
    For like the pendulum moving to and fro,
The paths are many I have still to go,
Knowing it was not me who set the springs,
That time and motion - they are celestial things.

My Dog

My dog is multilingual
My dog is mathematical
My dog is on top of life,
And doesn't need a sabbatical.

My neighbour was a good neighbour,
My neighbour was kind,
But my neighbour - when it came to dogs,
Was blind.

My dog's a hot dog
My dog is feisty
Two Alsations took a bite
And the vet's bill was tasty.

My dog can tell the time
It stands with expectation,
And sits with poise and without a noise,
Absorbed - in the chef's creation.

My dog is an ageing dog
The postman isn't sent away;
And there's no greeting at the door:
"I can't be bothered any more!"
My dog is ageing.

In Praise of the "Off" Switch

It's time to write a sonnet in your praise:
I've grappled with the subject now for days.
And as my head was flound'ring in the waves
I'd lose control, and grasp at what I craved.
    For in those moments, I was lost for words,
oblivious to the flight-paths of the birds,
for I was breathless, speechless at my craft;

72

A poet, without words, is simply daft.
   For poets do not give themselves to death,
no matter how they grieve or are bereft.
Knee deep in silt and filt'ring like a sieve,
they find the limpets - words by which they live.
      "My friend! Marconi! You are not to blame,
      that I should reach, for the "Off" switch, again"

Roots

1
Celebrity and freeman of the town
I am hell bent on rest and relaxation
of body and mind, while the blood
thickens, and the jaw freezes over.
Weighty minds lie still. And that
steady measure, that is progress,
is ignored - while I detox.

2
From the balcony I can look across
To the Devil's Washtub.

I cannot though, fathom its depth, nor hear
the head banging in its caverns.

But the pathways climbing to its summit
are clearly marked.

And though I cannot see, or hear it,
I know that the throat is convulsed.

3
Only the fabric of the once warring faiths
stands unscathed.

They say that, "time marches on", but not here
in these bedraggled streets.

The Crescent is toothless, the life
having gone from its mouth.

And the gulls, silent, sway, and muse
on the varicosed promenades.

There are people about, but their existence
seems hum drum.

So we must wait, and hope for an eruption
while the dead are clinging to life.

A Poem For My 69 th Birthday

Happiness

She has her room, and I have mine.
She has her computer, and I have mine.
She has friends, and I have none.
She has a way with numbers.
She has the gift of tongues.
She has a love of colour and flowers,
and is expert at food and wine, and *believes*
in consensus,
and minds the dishwasher.
I mind the dog,
the wheelie-bin
and garbage,
the hedge,
the hanging baskets
and fish.
And the teapot.
And thanks to her,
I am greatly improved.

Turning the Pages

"He's open to interpretation," which seems
the only sensible thing to say, in the absence of anything concrete.
Is he obscure because he is brilliant, or brilliant because he is obscure?
I knew a priest once, who was afraid of putting a book down,
                     in case it was something important.
A trick of the trade?
The writer gives the impression that he is a Catholic, and of Irish extraction,
and a scholar of weird and wonderful things, such as the boiling down of
                           St. Thomas Aquinas.
As yet, he hasn't said that he knows of the fate of St. John of the Cross,
but I am still turning the pages, surprised that I have come this far.
There is no Introduction, and no road map, which leaves me wondering if
I should exclude the notes from my soon to be published book.
On the face of it, I am tempted to argue that mine is better value.
But as his costs more, and is obscure, it could be the fruit of a good education.
So I won't start an argument, but opt instead, for reverence and respect.

Notes pp 10 -16

p.10 *"Miss Mills"* This poem is set against the backdrop of the sectarian and
tribal society of Northern Ireland, where Catholics and Protestants lived
separate lives. Miss Mills had been a member of the Salvation Army. By
marriage to Chris, a widower, Miss Mills became Mrs Johnson.

p.12 *"Who would be a girl when you can be a boy?"* From time-to-time the
"Royal Navy" would appear in the town, always in the summer months.
They would anchor in the bay just beyond Ramore Head

p.16 *"What will be will be"* Archbishop Godfrey of Liverpool, and his
successor, Archbishop Heenan, in turn became the Cardinal Archbishop
of Westminster. Sir Malcolm Sergeant was a guest of the adjudicator at a
singing competition at Rushworth & Drapers in Liverpool. A competition
in which I came second. As I remember it, I came one point behind the
winner. So I may have come first, had I not made the mistake of singing
the last line of each verse in the song, the same, when in fact, there was a
slight variation. This is what I remember of the song:
"Is it I wonder a rum thing,
or nothing to wonder upon?
That whenever a man's doing something,
There's always a boy looking on.
He may stand for hours like a dumb thing.
But this can be counted upon.
That wherever a man's doing something,
there's always a boy looking on."
Sir Charles Groves was Principal Conductor of the Royal Liverpool
Philharmonic Orchestra, and gave concerts for schools. St Vincent's
School is in the West Derby district of Liverpool. In my time there,
1954-58, it was run by the sisters of Charity of St Vincent de Paul. The
level of education provided was well below the norm for children of my
age. The nuns were aware of this, and tried to address the issue by
introducing Latin to the curriculum, for a select few of us; an experiment
which failed. This lagging behind, was in part due to the general
expectation of what could be achieved for children with disabilities. But
a further fact, was undoubtedly the nuns, who allowed their heart to rule
their heads. It was not in their nature to say no. Consequently, children
with multiple problems ended up at the school, and that, almost certainly
had a bearing on what was seen as possible.

N.B. This poem is personal to me, and it is not, either directly, or indirectly, to be interpreted as a statement about the school as it is today.

p.22 *"I did not say, and I would not say"* I have remembered the opening lines of the prayer quoted in the first stanza, from childhood. Though in the original draft, I used the word compelled rather than "impelled". The prayer was first read by Pope Pius XII in the Basilica of Santa Maria Maggiore in November 1950. A Holy Year. So I would have been eight at the time of this incident. My mother had returned earlier that day from a rare visit to my father's family. Sent to recover her Rosary from her coat pocket, and finding the money, I naively thought she had forgotten about it. So I took it, intending to give it to her later. But by the time the prayers were said, I had forgotten all about it. Almost certainly there were money problems, which was why she had gone to visit my father's family; and possibly at his bidding. In the circumstances, (my father was a binge drinker with a propensity to be violent when drunk), a sad fact of life was that there were things in the normal course of events that she would not have wanted him to know, and which we, as children were aware of. Additional money, as distinct from the "house keeping" that he doled out each week, was one of them. And I would not have understood, that in this instance, this was money that he knew about. The Rosary is a devotional exercise made up of fifteen mysteries They are split into three groups of five reflections on the life of Christ and wider Catholic belief. As mysteries they come under the headings of: Joyful, Sorrowful, and Glorious. And each of them are assigned to particular days of the week. Each of the mysteries are made up of five decades, a sequence of prayers that accompany each of the themes. As the poem makes reference to the Glorious mysteries, the themes are: The Resurrection (of Christ). The Ascension (Of Christ into Heaven), Pentecost (when the Holy Spirit descended on the Apostles in the upper room in Jerusalem). The Assumption of the Virgin Mary into Heaven). And, The Coronation (of the Virgin Mary in Heaven), which is a devotional rather than a literal concept).

p.25 *"Grandma"* The photograph of Grandma that accompanies my blog was taken by me in 1958, when I was 16. Grandma died in 1961 at the age of 93.

p.28 *"The Vigil"* I can't recall how many of these episodes I sat through.

Probably not that many. But the episode as described here, would have occurred in the winter months when we had no holidaymakers staying. As I left home to attend St. Vincent's in 1954, I would have been eleven at most, and possibly younger. I was definitely at primary school, as was Deirdre, who is mentioned in the poem.

p.33 _"From The Threshold"_ This poem tells the story of Bob, an odd job man in the Machine Shop, in Larne, where I had my first job. Frail (but still working in what was a cold and generally hostile environment), I was moved to ask him why he had not retired at 65. In reply, Bob told me that by working until he was 70 he would get a bigger pension. An explanation that I took at face value. But when he died, six weeks after he retired, I knew the truth. What had kept Bob at work was companionship and the feeling that he was needed. Hardly surprising, from this gentle man who had fought in both world wars.

p.34 _"Life"_ This poem is based on a Catholic family, with whom I lived for several months in Belfast. When Mary's husband left the army after 20 years, they embarked on a new life, with a new house and mortgage. Six weeks later, he drowned while on manoeuvres with the territorial army. Her son Bernard, who was a sea cadet and apprentice joiner, died from cancer of the spine at the age of 21. And not withstanding this tragedy and her husbands army career, and the fact that her oldest son was in the "British Army" in Germany, she had to flee with her remaining children when her home, along with others, was burned to the ground by a Loyalist mob.

p.37 _"The Victory" /_ " _"The Homecoming"_ both reflect on the 1998-99 football season, when Manchester United, (the first and only club in English football), to do so, won "the treble": The Premiership. The F.A. Cup, and the UEFA Champions League in the same season. They came from behind, in injury time, to beat Bayern Munich, 2-1. At that time, Jenny was living away from home, working in Norwich, which. from Leo's point of view added to the commotion and general excitement.

P46 _School_ "Who struck McCormack!" A greeting from the window cleaner, Jimmy Shaw, who in the first instance, left his ladder and popped across the street to school me in the answer. "The man with the caster hat!" I had no idea what it was all about. But it is a pleasant memory. "Cost a penny", alludes not just to the price but to what we called it. "The penny catechism" or "caddy." "Three into one did go." This references the doctrine of the Blessed Trinity. The poem, "Wander Thirst" is by Gerald Gould, which master Fitzpatrick brought to life by requiring me to recite to the class, gesticulating as appropriate.

p.49 *"My Sunflower Girl"* This poem was written for Jessica (Li Jie), when I thought that I had reason to be concerned for her. But as it turned out, the concerns were not justified.

p.50 *"For The Young"* This poem was composed against the backdrop of hostage taking in the Middle East and the unrestrained reporting of the more gruesome details. Reports that had no regard for the time of day, or the sensitivities or the vulnerabilities of the young

p.51 *"Liberation"* This poem is a response to the book, *Calvary In China,* by Robert W. Groene MM

p.53 *"Sinister Forces"* The backdrop to this poem is an IRA bombing campaign in England in the 1970s."pigs", slang for police.

p.54 *"Italy 2006"* Venice: The interior of St. Marks Cathedral. Florence: The area between the Cathedral and the Baptistery. Sienna: St. Catherine of Sienna. Rome: The Sistine Chapel. "Overrated and overstuffed"? As it was presented to the public, crowded and dark. And if it is the acclaimed masterpiece that it is supposed to be, why should people who have travelled across the world to see it, be reduced to silence. Especially when the chapel is not being used for religious ceremonies. "Temples": Churches. Some of which were modelled on the original Roman temples.

p.60 *"A Poem For My 66th Birthday"* "Sylvia": Sylvia Plath, American poet 1932-63. "Beyond Kinsale": a poem under construction. "Grecian Urn": "Ode on a Grecian Urn," by John Keats, 1795-1821. "Robert Frost": American Poet. 1874-1963 "Me!" The voice of Robert Frost. "Tulips": a poem by Sylvia Plath. "Alma Mater": The University of Liverpool, seeking a bequest (in my will), on the eve of my birthday! "When I have fears...", poem by John Keats

p.63 *"Trapped"* I was a lodger at Mrs. B's for six months in 1959: "A halfer". In this instance, a practicing Catholic, one of whose parents was a Protestant. Arthur's parents had come from England on a visit, and it was they who had told her that he would lose his inheritance. "The highest authority from England", alludes to the English Reformation. " Radio Eireann": Irish state radio, equivalent of the BBC."Eucharistic Congress": an international Roman Catholic celebration of religious faith.

The 31st international congress was held in Dublin in 1932

p.65 *"A Poem For My 67th Birthday"* The backdrop to this poem is the case of
Nigel Gresham who, inadvertently caused the deaths of 4 of his 7
children. The most famed story of the wisdom of King Solomon: The
Bible: Old Testament: Book of Kings Ch. 3. 16-28

"Lough Derg" This poem should be read in conjunction with my blog,
Anna's Postcard.

p.69 *"Making Mischief"* Vijay: Vijay Prakash. You have to be a connoisseur of
football to appreciate this poem, and to know how poorly Liverpool FC,
were doing when this poem was written in 2010. In the previous season,
2008-9, they finished as runners up to Manchester United. Unexpectedly
in the following year, they were in decline, failing to qualify for the play
off stages of the European Champions League; and were eighth in the
Premiership. An unprecedented state of affairs, given that in terms of the
end of season results, they were invariably one of "the big four." And
And there was well publicised disunity among the club's American
owners, which did not help. Stanza 1 An easy introduction with "gaffa"
a play on Rafa, and substitute for gaffe. 2 From this point on until the
final stanza, you only hear the voice of Sir Alex Ferguson, manager of
Liverpool's great rivals, Manchester United; and this stanza alludes to the
controversy surrounding Rafa's signings: as to how he did, or in some
cases, did not use them; something that not infrequently perplexed the
fans. 3 This stanza references the managers of Arsenal and Aston Villa
respectively, though Martin O'Neill is alluded to rather than named; and
it makes fun of Rafa's statement (after the club failed to qualify for the
play-off stages in the Champions League) that from Liverpool's point of
view, "the season begins now"! 4 You can't poke fun at Liverpool's
misfortune without mentioning Everton and their manager David Moyes
as they too belong to the city of Liverpool. 5 Here to some extent the
tables are turned, with fun being poked at Sir Alex Ferguson who is
notorious for pointing at his watch, and by inference, at the referee in
respect of the amount of "extra time" that is, or is not allowed in any
given match. Hence, "The referees know I am willing." But it is a short
lived distraction, for in conclusion we are reminded of Rafa's Rant,
when in the 2008-9 season at a press conference he produced a note
criticising Sir Alex Ferguson and the Football Association for their
deferential attitude to him. And "thrilling" reminds us that it was Sir

Alex and not Rafa who triumphed in the end. 6 This is the only point in
the poem when you hear Rafa, but speaking only through Sir Alex, who,
in the language of Robert Burns, (and after an implied interruption),
advises him to leave Liverpool. Such is the pressure, that Rafa has
forgotten that Carlos Tevez no longer plays for Manchester United, but
Manchester City.

p.71 *"A Poem For My 68th Birthday"* References. Shakespeare. Song: The
Three Ravens, in which the "faithful hawks" guard the dead body of the
knight from the ravens: birds of prey. "In life, in epitaph ...", my own
poems "tigerish" my birthday coinciding with Chinese New Year: the
year of the tiger. "hors-d'oeuvre" the appetiser or medications that set me
up for the day.

p.72 *"My Dog"* This poem was written in conjunction with my blog, "What's
in a Dog."

p.73 *"Roots"* These poems first appeared in my blog, *Roots*

Index of first lines: